# Who's a Clever Baby then?

# Who's a Clever Baby then?

*Per i nonni*
*Mario e Luisa*

A Red Fox Book

Published by Random House Children's Books
20 Vauxhall Bridge Road, London SW1V 2SA

A division of Random House UK Ltd
London Melbourne Sydney Auckland
Johannesburg and agencies throughout the world
First published in 1988 by Andersen Press
Beaver edition 1990
Red Fox edition 1995

3 5 7 9 10 8 6 4

Printed in Hong Kong

RANDOM HOUSE UK Limited Reg. No. 954009

ISBN 0 09 965020 7

# Who's a Clever Baby then?

David McKee

Red Fox

"Who's a clever baby then?" said Grandma. "And where's my oofum boofum pussy cat? Say 'cat', Baby."

"Dog," said Baby.

"Oh Baby, look at the tiger, just look at the tiger," said Grandma. "Oh what terrible teeth has Trevor the television tiger. Say 'tiger', Baby."

"Dog," said Baby.

"Oh come on, Baby," said Grandma. "Let's feed Freddy, the funny fat freckled fish. Say 'fish', Baby."

"Dog," said Baby.

"Oh Baby, look there," said Grandma. "See the birds? The big brown birds biting Beryl's beautiful blue berries. Say 'bird', Baby."

"Dog," said Baby.

"Oh my. Oh my. Look at the teddies, Baby," said Grandma. "There are fat teddies and tall teddies, thin teddies and small teddies, young teddies and old teddies, curly teddies and bald teddies. Pink teddies and blue teddies, and some bigger-than-you teddies. Say 'teddy', Baby."

"Dog," said Baby.

"Oh Baby," said Grandma. "There's Peter and
Pamela Pointer packing a perfect painting of a
pretty pink paddling penguin. Say 'penguin', Baby."
   "Dog," said Baby.

"Oh Baby," said Grandma. "See the statue? See strong Samson silently struggling with Simon, the serious stone lion. Say 'lion', Baby."

"Dog," said Baby.

"Oh ho. Oh ho, Baby," said Grandma. "There's another baby, Baby. A lovely wovely baby, Baby, an oochy coochy baby, Baby. And where's my clever wever baby, Baby? Say 'baby', Baby."

"Dog," said Baby.

"Up Baby, down Baby, to Baby and fro Baby.
Rumpity rumpity rumpity rump," said Grandma.
"Does the clever baby like Edward, the enormous
electric elephant, then? Say 'elephant', Baby."

"Dog," said Baby.

"Oh, hey, Baby," said Grandma. "Look at the clockwork crocodile. It's a cheerful crocodile, a creeping crocodile, a clicking crocodile, a crazy crimson-coloured crocodile. Say 'crocodile', Baby."

"Dog," said Baby.

"Oh ha ha ha," laughed Grandma. "Oh ha ha ha. Oh look, Baby. Ha ha ha, look at the horse, Baby. Oh he he he. Oh what a comical clowning circus horse. Oh ho ho ho. Oh what a handsome happy humorous horse. Oh ha ha ha. Say 'horse', Baby."

"Dog," said Baby.

"Oh Baby, who's a clever baby then?" said Grandma. "Look, my clever baby, there's a big booful wooful doggie woggie for my clever wever baby. Such a darling dog, Baby. Who's a clever baby then? Say 'dog', Baby."

"Cat," said Baby.

# Some bestselling Red Fox picture books

THE BIG ALFIE AND ANNIE ROSE STORYBOOK
*by Shirley Hughes*
OLD BEAR
*by Jane Hissey*
OI! GET OFF OUR TRAIN
*by John Burningham*
DON'T DO THAT!
*by Tony Ross*
NOT NOW, BERNARD
*by David McKee*
ALL JOIN IN
*by Quentin Blake*
THE WHALES' SONG
*by Gary Blythe and Dyan Sheldon*
JESUS' CHRISTMAS PARTY
*by Nicholas Allan*
THE PATCHWORK CAT
*by Nicola Bayley and William Mayne*
WILLY AND HUGH
*by Anthony Browne*
THE WINTER HEDGEHOG
*by Ann and Reg Cartwright*
A DARK, DARK TALE
*by Ruth Brown*
HARRY, THE DIRTY DOG
*by Gene Zion and Margaret Bloy Graham*
DR XARGLE'S BOOK OF EARTHLETS
*by Jeanne Willis and Tony Ross*
WHERE'S THE BABY?
*by Pat Hutchins*